This Absurdly Easy Gratitude Journal Belongs To:

Gratitude is magic, for real. But sometimes the idea of keeping a "gratitude list" feels like it'd be hard, like it'd be too much work...which is weird, because gratitude is easy. Like, crazy-easy. That's what this easy-peasy little journal is all about! All you do is think of one thing you're thankful for. One thing. It can be something tiny, like the veins in a leaf, or something super mundane, like a mega-roll of toilet paper. We can't explain how the magic works, but it's pretty much the quickest way to feel better about your life. Even the most boring or bummer days contain something worth celebrating. (Or at least like 98% of them do.) Sometimes, just brushing your teeth is an act of heroism! Some days, the greatest thing that ever happened is that bowl of mac & cheese you had at 10:30 pm. Praise and honor your mac & cheese moments as well as your swimming-with-dolphins-in-the-ocean days! Don't be afraid to list the same thing more than once or twice or whatever. Feel free to rewrite any of the prompts as you see fit. And if you ever get stumped, here are some suggestions:

The smell of coffee, rain, old books

Seeing a butterfly land on a flower

Pizza. Popcorn. Tacos!

Treehouses

Fuzzy socks

Your favorite TV show, movie, song

Your happiest happy place

A flower growing through a crack in the sidewalk

That lady at the drive-thru who called you "Hon"

The fact that tomorrow's a new day

Health (yours or someone else's)

The stars and moon

Sleep

The taste of water

Your funniest memory

Someone who once helped you

Your good taste in shoes/music/whatever

The library

Baby hedgehogs, kittens, puppies!

Birds singing at night

The kindness of strangers

The smell of a newborn baby

Being able to read and write

Morning sunshine on your back

Running into a dear old friend when you feel lonely

Finding money in a pocket

A pretty good hair day

The desire to do better next time

The best thing that ever happened to me today:

The best thing that ever happened to me today:

The best thing that ever happened to me today:

The best thing I ever ate today:

DATE
/   /

_____

_____

_____

_____

_____

_____

The best thing that ever happened to me today:

DATE
/   /

_____

_____

_____

_____

_____

_____

The best thing that ever happened to me today:

DATE
/   /

_____

_____

_____

_____

_____

_____

☐ *I'm the best thing that happened today!*

The best thing that ever happened to me today:

The most fun I ever had today:

The best thing that ever happened to me today:

The best thing that ever happened to me today:

The best thing that ever happened to me today:

The best thing that ever happened to me today:

☐ *And I deserve a bunch more of this sort of thing!*

The most beautiful thing I ever saw today:

The best thing that ever happened to me today:

The best thing that ever happened to me today:

The best thing that ever happened to me today:

The best thing that ever happened to me today:

The best thing that ever happened to me today:

☐ #truestory

The best thing that ever happened to me today:

_____

_____

_____

_____

_____

_____

The best thing that ever happened to me today:

_____

_____

_____

_____

_____

_____

The least-crappy thing that ever happened to me today:

_____

_____

_____

_____

_____

_____

The best thing that ever happened to me today:

_____

_____

_____

_____

_____

_____

The best thing that ever happened to me today:

_____

_____

_____

_____

_____

_____

The best thing that ever happened to me today:

_____

_____

_____

_____

_____

_____

☐ *Yay, me!*

The best thing that ever happened to me today:

_____

_____

_____

_____

_____

_____

The best thing that ever happened to me today:

_____

_____

_____

_____

_____

_____

The best thing that ever happened to me today:

_____

_____

_____

_____

_____

_____

The best thing that ever happened to me today: DATE / /

_____

_____

_____

_____

_____

_____

The best thing that ever happened to me today: DATE / /

_____

_____

_____

_____

_____

_____

The best thing that ever made me think people don't suck today: DATE / /

_____

_____

_____

_____

_____

☐ *Wow, I totally don't suck at all.*

The best thing that ever happened to me today:

The best news I ever heard today:

The best thing that ever happened to me today:

The best thing that ever happened to me today:

The best thing that ever happened to me today:

The best thing that ever happened to me today:

☐ *Looks in mirror: "Hey, cutie!"*

The best thing that ever happened to me today:

The best thing that ever happened to me today:

The best thing that ever happened to me today:

The most happy-making thing that ever happened today:

DATE
/   /

The best thing that ever happened to me today:

DATE
/   /

The best thing that ever happened to me today:

DATE
/   /

☐ *Bring on the good stuff!*

The best thing that ever happened to me today:

The best thing that ever happened to me today:

The best thing that ever happened to me today:

The coolest tree, flower, or plant I ever saw today:

DATE
/   /

The best thing that ever happened to me today:

DATE
/   /

The best thing that ever happened to me today:

DATE
/   /

☐ *I'm on a strict no-BS plan.*

The best thing that ever happened to me today:

The kindest self-caring thing I ever did today:

The best thing that ever happened to me today:

The best thing that ever happened to me today:

The best thing that ever happened to me today:

The best thing that ever happened to me today:

☐ *I was also the best me that happened today.*

The best thing that ever happened to me today:

_____

_____

_____

_____

_____

_____

_____

The best thing that ever happened to me today:

_____

_____

_____

_____

_____

_____

_____

The best thing that ever happened to me today:

_____

_____

_____

_____

_____

_____

_____

The best thing that ever happened to me today:

DATE / /

The best human or animal friend I ever had today:

DATE / /

The best thing that ever happened to me today:

DATE / /

☐ _Cute outfit!_

The best thing that ever happened to me today:

The best thing that ever happened to me today:

The best thing that ever happened to me today:

The nicest thing that ever happened to me today:

DATE

/   /

The best thing that ever happened to me today:

DATE

/   /

The best thing that ever happened to me today:

DATE

/   /

☐ *Well done.*

The best thing that ever happened to me today:

DATE
/   /

The best thing that ever happened to me today:

DATE
/   /

The best thing that ever happened to me today:

DATE
/   /

The body part I feel the most thankful ever for today:

DATE

/   /

The best thing that ever happened to me today:

DATE

/   /

The best thing that ever happened to me today:

DATE

/   /

☐ *I am enough just as I am.*

The best thing that ever happened to me today:

The best thing that ever happened to me today:

The best thing that ever happened to me today:

The best thing that ever happened to me today:

The most profound love I ever felt today:

The best thing that ever happened to me today:

☐ *It's OK to not be OK!*

The best thing I ever saw while looking up today:

DATE
/ /

The best thing that ever happened to me today:

DATE
/ /

The best thing that ever happened to me today:

DATE
/ /

The best thing that ever happened to me today:

DATE / /

The best thing that ever happened to me today:

DATE / /

The best thing that ever happened to me today:

DATE / /

☐ *Stay gold, champ!*

The best thing that ever happened to me today:

The best thing that ever happened to me today:

The best thing that ever happened to me today:

The most my-best-self thing I ever did today:

DATE
/   /

The best thing that ever happened to me today:

DATE
/   /

The best thing that ever happened to me today:

DATE
/   /

☐ *I got this.*

The best thing that ever happened to me today: DATE
                                                                    /   /

The best thing that ever happened to me today: DATE
                                                                    /   /

The best thing that ever happened to me today: DATE
                                                                    /   /

The best thing that ever happened to me today:

DATE
/   /

The most inspiring daydream I ever had today:

DATE
/   /

The best thing that ever happened to me today:

DATE
/   /

☐ *Bring it on, baby.*

The best thing that ever happened to me today:

The best thing that ever happened to me today:

The most comforting thing I ever heard today:

The best thing that ever happened to me today:

The best thing that ever happened to me today:

The best thing that ever happened to me today:

☐ *I am loved.*

The best thing that ever happened to me today:

_____

_____

_____

_____

_____

_____

The best thing that ever happened to me today:

_____

_____

_____

_____

_____

_____

The best thing that ever happened to me today:

_____

_____

_____

_____

_____

_____

The best thing that ever happened to me today:

The most forgiving thought I ever had (about me or someone else) today:

The best thing that ever happened to me today:

☐ _Keep on keepin' on!_

The best thing that ever happened to me today:

The most magical-est thing that ever happened today:

The best thing that ever happened to me today:

The best thing that ever happened to me today:

The best thing that ever happened to me today:

The best thing that ever happened to me today:

☐ *High fives for me!*

The best thing that ever happened to me today:

DATE
/   /

_____

_____

_____

_____

_____

_____

The best thing that ever happened to me today:

DATE
/   /

_____

_____

_____

_____

_____

_____

The wisest thing my gut ever told me today:

DATE
/   /

_____

_____

_____

_____

_____

_____

The best thing that ever happened to me today:

DATE
/   /

The best thing that ever happened to me today:

DATE
/   /

The best thing that ever happened to me today:

DATE
/   /

☐ *Me for the win!*

The best thing that ever happened to me today:

_____

_____

_____

_____

_____

_____

The best thing that ever happened to me today:

_____

_____

_____

_____

_____

_____

The best thing that ever happened to me today:

_____

_____

_____

_____

_____

_____

The best thing that ever happened to me today:

The best thing that ever happened to me today:

The most-annoying-thing-ever I did NOT have to do today (yay!):

☐ *Oh yeah, I'm #goals!*

The best thing that ever happened to me today:

The best thing that ever happened to me today:

The best thing that ever happened to me today:

The most amazing insight I ever had today:

The best thing that ever happened to me today:

The best thing that ever happened to me today:

☐ *Can't stop, won't stop.*

The best thing that ever happened to me today:

The best thing that ever happened to me today:

The most creative little (or big) thing I ever did today:

The best thing that ever happened to me today:

The best thing that ever happened to me today:

The best thing that ever happened to me today:

☐ *Not to brag, but I'm pretty good at this.*

The best thing that ever happened to me today:

The best tiny little accomplishment I ever had today:

The best thing that ever happened to me today:

The best thing that ever happened to me today:

The best thing that ever happened to me today:

The best thing that ever happened to me today:

☐ *I'm a beautiful work in progress.*

The best thing that ever happened to me today:

The best thing that ever happened to me today:

The best thing that ever happened to me today:

The best thing that ever happened to me today:

The healthiest thing I ever did (or didn't do!) today:

The best thing that ever happened to me today:

☐ _XOXO to me!_

The thing that gave me the most hope ever today:

The best thing that ever happened to me today:

The best thing that ever happened to me today:

The best thing that ever happened to me today:

The best thing that ever happened to me today:

The best thing that ever happened to me today:

☐ *I'm kinda sorta crushin' it.*

The thing that gave me the best little ray of sunshine ever today:

The best thing that ever happened to me today:

The best thing that ever happened to me today:

The best thing that ever happened to me today:

_____

_____

_____

_____

_____

_____

_____

The best thing that ever happened to me today:

_____

_____

_____

_____

_____

_____

_____

The best thing that ever happened to me today:

_____

_____

_____

_____

_____

_____

☐ *Just over here bringing the gratitude.*

The best thing that ever happened to me today:

The best thing that ever happened to me today:

The best thing that ever happened to me today:

The best treat I ever gave myself today:

The best thing that ever happened to me today:

The best thing that ever happened to me today:

☐ *Straight fire, that's me!*

The best thing that ever happened to me today:

_____

_____

_____

_____

_____

_____

The best thing that ever happened to me today:

_____

_____

_____

_____

_____

_____

The best thing that ever happened to me today:

_____

_____

_____

_____

_____

_____

The best thing that ever happened to me today:

The best thing that ever happened to me today:

The best thing I ever learned today:

☐ *I'm a keeper!*

The best thing that ever happened to me today:

The best thing that ever happened to me today:

The best thing that ever happened to me today:

The best thing that ever happened to me today:

The greatest small/huge decision I made today:

The best thing that ever happened to me today:

☐ *I've got a heart of gold.*

The best thing that ever happened to me today:

The best thing that ever happened to me today:

The omg-est thing that ever happened to me today:

The best thing that ever happened to me today:

The best thing that ever happened to me today:

The best thing that ever happened to me today:

☐ *I'm the best thing that happened today!*

The best thing that ever happened to me today:

/   /

_____
_____
_____
_____
_____
_____
_____

The best thing that ever happened to me today:

/   /

_____
_____
_____
_____
_____
_____
_____

The best thing that ever happened to me today:

/   /

_____
_____
_____
_____
_____
_____
_____

The best thing that ever happened to me today:

DATE
/ /

_____

_____

_____

_____

_____

_____

The best thing that ever happened to me today:

DATE
/ /

_____

_____

_____

_____

_____

_____

The most heart-opening thing that ever happened today:

DATE
/ /

_____

_____

_____

_____

_____

_____

☐ *And I deserve a bunch more of this sort of thing!*

The best thing that ever happened to me today:

The best thing that ever happened to me today:

The best compliment I ever got (or gave!) today:

The best thing that ever happened to me today:

The best thing that ever happened to me today:

The best thing that ever happened to me today:

☐ *#truestory*

The best thing that ever happened to me today:

DATE
/   /

_____

_____

_____

_____

_____

_____

_____

The best thing that ever happened to me today:

DATE
/   /

_____

_____

_____

_____

_____

_____

_____

The best thing that ever happened to me today:

DATE
/   /

_____

_____

_____

_____

_____

_____

The best thing that ever happened to me today:

The best memory I ever remembered today:

The best thing that ever happened to me today:

☐ *Yay, me!*

The mightiest baby step I ever took today:

DATE

/   /

The best thing that ever happened to me today:

DATE

/   /

The best thing that ever happened to me today:

DATE

/   /

The best thing that ever happened to me today:

The best thing that ever happened to me today:

The best thing that ever happened to me today:

☐ *Wow, I totally don't suck at all.*

The best thing that ever happened to me today:

_____

_____

_____

_____

_____

_____

The best thing that ever happened to me today:

_____

_____

_____

_____

_____

_____

The best thing that ever happened to me today:

_____

_____

_____

_____

_____

_____

The cutest living thing I ever saw today:

The best thing that ever happened to me today:

The best thing that ever happened to me today:

□ *Looks in mirror: "Hey, cutie!"*

The best thing that ever happened to me today:

The best thing that ever happened to me today:

The most awesome thing I ever did today:

The best thing that ever happened to me today:

The best thing that ever happened to me today:

The best thing that ever happened to me today:

☐ *Bring on the good stuff!*

The best thing that ever happened to me today:

The best thing that ever happened to me today:

The best thing that ever happened to me today:

The best thing that ever happened to me today: DATE
                                                                    /   /

_____

_____

_____

_____

_____

_____

The best thing that ever happened to me today: DATE
                                                                    /   /

_____

_____

_____

_____

_____

_____

The best wish I ever made that might come true—someday!—today: DATE
                                                                    /   /

_____

_____

_____

_____

_____

☐ *I'm on a strict no-BS plan.*

The best thing that ever happened to me today:

DATE
/   /

The best thing that ever happened to me today:

DATE
/   /

The best thing that ever happened to me today:

DATE
/   /

The best thing that ever happened to me today:

The raddest thing that ever happened to me today:

The best thing that ever happened to me today:

☐ *I was also the best me that happened today.*

The most delicious scent I ever smelled today:

The best thing that ever happened to me today:

The best thing that ever happened to me today:

The best thing that ever happened to me today:

The best thing that ever happened to me today:

The best thing that ever happened to me today:

☐ *Cute outfit!*

The best thing that ever happened to me today:

The best thing that ever happened to me today:

My most-favorite thing that ever happened today:

The best thing that ever happened to me today:

_____

_____

_____

_____

_____

_____

The best thing that ever happened to me today:

_____

_____

_____

_____

_____

_____

The best thing that ever happened to me today:

_____

_____

_____

_____

_____

_____

☐ *Well done.*

The best thing that ever happened to me today:

The most fun-to-think-about scheme I ever hatched today:

The best thing that ever happened to me today:

The best thing that ever happened to me today:

The best thing that ever happened to me today:

The best thing that ever happened to me today:

☐ *I am enough just as I am.*

The best thing that ever happened to me today:

DATE
/   /

The best thing that ever happened to me today:

DATE
/   /

The funniest thing I ever heard today:

DATE
/   /

The best thing that ever happened to me today:

_____

_____

_____

_____

_____

_____

The best thing that ever happened to me today:

_____

_____

_____

_____

_____

_____

The best thing that ever happened to me today:

_____

_____

_____

_____

_____

_____

☐ *It's OK to not be OK!*

The best thing that ever happened to me today:

The best thing that ever happened to me today:

The best thing that ever happened to me today:

The best thing that ever happened to me today:

The best thing that ever happened to me today:

The best thing I ever saw while looking down today:

☐ *Stay gold, champ!*

The best thing that ever happened to me today:

_____

_____

_____

_____

_____

_____

_____

The sweetest simple pleasure I ever had today:

_____

_____

_____

_____

_____

_____

_____

The best thing that ever happened to me today:

_____

_____

_____

_____

_____

_____

The best thing that ever happened to me today:

DATE
/   /

_____

_____

_____

_____

_____

_____

The best thing that ever happened to me today:

DATE
/   /

_____

_____

_____

_____

_____

_____

The best thing that ever happened to me today:

DATE
/   /

_____

_____

_____

_____

_____

_____

☐ *I got this.*

The silliest worry I ever released today:

The best thing that ever happened to me today:

The best thing that ever happened to me today:

The best thing that ever happened to me today:

The best thing that ever happened to me today:

The best thing that ever happened to me today:

☐ *Bring it on, baby.*

The best thing that ever happened to me today:

The best thing that ever happened to me today:

The best thing that ever happened to me today:

The best thing that ever happened to me today: DATE
                                                                   /   /

_____

_____

_____

_____

_____

_____

The greatest human I ever knew today: DATE
                                                                   /   /

_____

_____

_____

_____

_____

_____

The best thing that ever happened to me today: DATE
                                                                   /   /

_____

_____

_____

_____

_____

_____

☐ *I am loved.*

The most joyful moment I ever had today:

DATE

/   /

_____

_____

_____

_____

_____

_____

The best thing that ever happened to me today:

DATE

/   /

_____

_____

_____

_____

_____

_____

The best thing that ever happened to me today:

DATE

/   /

_____

_____

_____

_____

_____

_____

The best thing that ever happened to me today:

_____

_____

_____

_____

_____

_____

The best thing that ever happened to me today:

_____

_____

_____

_____

_____

_____

The best thing that ever happened to me today:

_____

_____

_____

_____

_____

_____

☐ *Keep on keepin' on!*

The best thing that ever happened to me today:

DATE
/   /

The best thing that ever happened to me today:

DATE
/   /

The best thing that ever happened to me today:

DATE
/   /

The best thing that ever happened to me today:

The best thing that ever happened to me today:

The coziest nook I was ever in today:

☐ *High fives for me!*

The best thing that ever happened to me today:

The best thing that ever happened to me today:

The best thing that ever happened to me today:

The best thing that ever made me wanna cry (in a good way) today: DATE
                                                                        /   /

_____

_____

_____

_____

_____

_____

The best thing that ever happened to me today: DATE
                                                   /   /

_____

_____

_____

_____

_____

_____

The best thing that ever happened to me today: DATE
                                                   /   /

_____

_____

_____

_____

_____

_____

☐ *Me for the win!*

The best thing that ever happened to me today:

DATE
/   /

The best good-weird thing that ever happened to me today:

DATE
/   /

The best thing that ever happened to me today:

DATE
/   /

The best thing that ever happened to me today:

DATE
/   /

The best thing that ever happened to me today:

DATE
/   /

The best thing that ever happened to me today:

DATE
/   /

☐ *Oh yeah, I'm #goals!*

The best thing that ever happened to me today: DATE   /   /

The best thing that ever happened to me today: DATE   /   /

The best thing that ever happened to me today: DATE   /   /

The best thing that ever happened to me today:

The best conversation I ever had today:

The best thing that ever happened to me today:

☐ *Can't stop, won't stop.*

The best thing that ever made me smile today:

/ /

The best thing that ever happened to me today:

DATE
/ /

The best thing that ever happened to me today:

DATE
/ /

The best thing that ever happened to me today:

The best thing that ever happened to me today:

The best thing that ever happened to me today:

☐ *Not to brag, but I'm pretty good at this.*

The best thing that ever happened to me today:

The best thing that ever happened to me today:

The best thing that ever happened to me today:

The best thing that ever happened to me today:

The best thing that ever happened to me today:

The crappiest feeling I ever said "No" to today:

☐ *I'm a beautiful work in progress.*

The best advice I ever got (or gave!) today:

The best thing that ever happened to me today:

The best thing that ever happened to me today:

The best thing that ever happened to me today:

The best thing that ever happened to me today:

The best thing that ever happened to me today:

☐ *XOXO to me!*

The best thing that ever happened to me today:

The best thing that ever happened to me today:

The best thing that ever happened to me today:

The most awesome song lyrics I ever remembered today:　　　　　DATE
/　/

The best thing that ever happened to me today:　　　　　DATE
/　/

The best thing that ever happened to me today:　　　　　DATE
/　/

☐ *I'm kinda sorta crushin' it.*

The best thing that ever happened to me today:

The best thing that ever happened to me today:

The best thing that ever happened to me today:

The best thing that ever happened to me today:

The best thing I ever overheard someone say today:

The best thing that ever happened to me today:

☐ _Just over here bringing the gratitude._

The best thing that ever happened to me today:

DATE
/   /

The most awesome random thing that ever happened today:

DATE
/   /

The best thing that ever happened to me today:

DATE
/   /

The best thing that ever happened to me today:

The best thing that ever happened to me today:

The best thing that ever happened to me today:

☐ *Straight fire, that's me!*

The best thing that ever happened to me today:

The best thing that ever happened to me today:

The best thing that ever happened to me today:

The most carefree moment I ever had today:

The best thing that ever happened to me today:

The best thing that ever happened to me today:

☐ *I'm a keeper!*

The coolest thing that ever happened to me today:

The best thing that ever happened to me today:

The best thing that ever happened to me today:

The best thing that ever happened to me today:

The best thing that ever happened to me today:

The best thing that ever happened to me today:

☐ *I've got a heart of gold.*

The best thing that ever happened to me today:

_____

_____

_____

_____

_____

_____

The best thing that ever happened to me today:

_____

_____

_____

_____

_____

_____

The best thing that ever happened to me today:

_____

_____

_____

_____

_____

_____

The best thing that ever happened to me today:

The best thing that ever happened to me today:

The best thing I'm looking forward to tomorrow:

☐ *I'm the best thing that happened today!*

REFLECTIONS ON MY
YEAR-OR-SO OF BEST-EVER THINGS

How did I feel when I started?

☐ *Kinda optimistic!*   ☐ *Kinda skeptical.*   ☐ *Kinda goofy.*

☐

How do I feel now?

☐ *Grateful.*   ☐ *Super grateful.*   ☐ *Grateful it's over!*

☐

Something I learned about myself:

☐ *I'm pretty lucky.*   ☐ *I'm pretty loopy.*   ☐ *I'm pretty lazy.*

☐

Funniest thing I was ever grateful for:

Best-est lesson I was ever grateful for:

Most surprising thing I was ever grateful for:

Littlest thing I was ever grateful for:

Biggest thing I was ever grateful for:

Overall best thing that ever happened:

A time this gratitude journal really helped me:

Has this whole gratitude thing changed me or my life?

Oh yeah, and also:

– You're the Best Ever! –

THANK YOU!